MW01127291

CAN I

INDEPENDENT PUBLISHING

PICK

LESSONS, TIPS

YOUR

AND STORIES

BRAIN?

Carlos Harleaux

Shawna,
Thank you so much
for your support!
I hope you enjoy the
book!

Carlos Harleaux

Can I Pick Your Brain?
Copyright ©2023 by Carlos Harleaux.

Published by 7th Sign Publishing
(peauxeticexpressions.com)

All rights reserved. No part of this book may be reproduced or transmitted
in any form or by any means without written permission from the author/
and or publisher.

ISBN 9798218084417
Book Cover Design by Matt Davies
Typesetting by Stewart A. Williams
Photography by Chris Booth

CONTENTS

Introduction

Malcom Gladwell, one of my favorite authors, stated in his book, *Outliers*, that it takes 10,000 hours (or approximately 10 years) of experience or deliberate practice to become an expert at a given skill or trade. Although I wouldn't consider myself an expert (the term is cringe-worthy to me), I can easily check the 10 years of experience box. I started 7th Sign Publishing in 2013, as a professional moniker for the publishing of my own books. More importantly, I desired to help other indie authors turn their stories into tangible (or digital) books.

The decision to start a publishing company didn't happen overnight. After self-publishing my first book, *Blurred Vision*, in 2011, many people asked me how I did it. The questions would always start with, "Can I pick your brain?" The wealth of information wasn't as vast back then. If you wanted to publish your own book, you really had to do your research. Today, there are countless resources available to indie authors, including YouTube videos, free workshops, podcasts, and social media profiles that give you the step-by-step breakdown to move your thoughts from pen to paper (or fingertips to laptop).

Even after publishing over 25 of my own books and books for others, I always learn something new.

Every.

Single.

Time.

The lessons I've learned over the last 10 years are what shaped this book. Experience may be the best teacher but there are some lessons we can avoid learning by taking notes from others. *Can I*

Pick Your Brain? is part instructional manual, part personal experiences (I love a good story) and all heart.

My prayer is that anyone reading this book finds it informative, entertaining, thought-provoking and trailblazing to start that fire within to make your own dreams a reality. Let the brain picking begin. Here's the good, the bad and the downright ugly of my experience with publishing over the last 10 years.

CHAPTER ONE

You Never Forget Your First

Imagine the taste of your first kiss (pretend it was amazing, even if it wasn't). The first bite of a decadent meal. The freeing euphoria of freedom after feeling caged.

Yep.

Your first book is like all these moments. I've written 15 books to date and none of my releases have felt quite like the feeling of holding my first book in my hand.

Let's rewind a bit.

The first time I seriously thought about publishing a book of poetry was around 2004. I held on to the concept and the title (*Blurred Vision*) for several years until I made the great leap of faith. The first jump is always the hardest. Many people ask me how to get started with a book and they don't realize they've just answered their own question.

Start.

That's it.

Ok, so maybe it's not quite that simple. One proven method that has worked for me is putting myself in an environment that's creatively conducive for my writing. The space doesn't have to mean you always leave home or go to some exotic island to get-away (but of course, that's great too). It's whatever makes you feel at your best when you write.

I love listening to some great music (Erykah Badu, Jill Scott, Pink and Maroon 5 always win for me) with some candles and maybe a glass of wine. Starbucks is one of my favorite places to write novels, especially pre-pandemic. I usually sit in a corner with my headphones and my tea (I don't drink coffee) and people-watch as I type out the details of my story on the computer. Some of the story lines in my books have come from true events with a twist but many of them have simply come from watching strangers interact.

Find your groove, whatever and wherever it leads you. However, I'll say that it's always great to be flexible enough for new methods of writing. I credit Akela Renae, my friend and co-author of *Only for One Night,* for pushing me to create a detailed outline for a novel. I always had a rough outline in my head before we collaborated. I knew the beginning, middle, and end. All I had to do was fill in the gaps. That was not the method when I worked with Akela. She suggested (and I grudgingly agreed) that we outline every chapter of the book. So, we did just that. We brainstormed about the characters and who would do what.

The outline was grueling at times. However, it was something that had to be done for two writers contributing to one book. I approached all my novels with an outline after my writing experience with Akela. You never stop learning and growing in publishing and writing. Once I gave in to the concept of the outline, writing each chapter became less stressful because the bones were solid.

Looking back, I had a slew of excuses that held me back from publishing my first book. Thankfully, poetry is one of the easiest genres to write. It's one of those creative outlets that is best explained by the author but open to interpretation by anyone who reads the work. I had a stack of poems to choose from, over 200 to be exact. That part came easily. I even had the conceptual design of the book cover in my head.

First came the fear that people wouldn't like my poems. I mean, after all, who was I to think someone could pick up my poetry book after reading works from internationally renowned poets such as Maya Angelou or Edgar Allen Poe? The sheer audacity of it all made me hesitant to move forward. Fear is a crippling emotion that can motivate us and stifle our growth all at once. Believe me, I understand. Even now, I'm always nervous right before a book is released. I'm not extremely concerned with how many books I sell, but I do want anyone who reads one of my books to enjoy it and understand the content.

Then, there was the fear of rejection from traditional publishers. Back then (and to some extent even now), most traditional publishers wouldn't touch you without the tiresome legwork of a literary agent who made your book appear compelling enough for consideration. Let's not forget that poetry used to be an incredibly hard market to break through barriers. It's one of those genres that people think is sexy enough to discuss at dinner but not enticing enough to dig in their pockets and purchase. I started researching anything I could find online about the benefits of self-publishing vs. traditional publishing. In short, it's a much greater hustle to self-publish but the return can be quicker and often greater than what you receive through a traditional publishing contract. I'll get into more of that later.

Finally, there was the elusive elephant in the room: money.

Whew.

Money was the certainly the biggest excuse that reared its ugly head each time I made progress towards publishing *Blurred Vision*. However, after a nice work bonus for an out-of-state training for several months for my 9 to 5, I received all of the money I need to publish my first book…..and then some.

There were no more excuses.

Part of the reason why it took me so long to publish my first book was because I wanted to know that it was real. I wanted to make sure that my desire to get involved in something that would ultimately require many sleepless nights, unwavering decisions and vulnerability wouldn't leave me with countless pages of regret. One sure sign that you are walking in your purpose is when something nags you. When you go to bed with it on your mind, wake up with it at the top of the day and maybe get a tad bit distracted from your day job thinking about it, you're supposed to do it.

So, I forged ahead. I dove in headfirst to find a book cover designer and an editor. Those were two major things I saw repeatedly in my research. Almost all the information I found stated how important the look of the book cover is to the sales of your book. Plus, editing was a huge component because after all, no one wants to read a book full of grammatical errors. Ironically, I have found errors in traditionally published books over the years. Nevertheless, we all want the least number of errors humanly possible.

Another positive about poetry is the editing process isn't the same as a novel or educational literary work. The genre can gauge the scope of work needed for an editor and which type of editor you'll need. Authors are artists at their core. As the great Erykah Badu stated on her hit song, "Tyrone", those artists are "sensitive about their ish". That means that most authors think their paintings are masterpieces. I'm not excluded from that number.

Nonetheless, all the technical pieces to constructing your first published book should be cherished. Things moved very quickly after I released *Blurred Vision*. I signed up for more vendor events, promoted heavily and oh, did I say promoted heavily (we'll talk more about that later too)?

I don't live with regrets for most situations. Everything happens for a reason and if I adjusted moments in time, I probably wouldn't be who I am today (maybe for better or worse). One regret I do have is I would have cherished the moments of having my first book published and in-hand.

As a writer, you often feel like you must pinch yourself to believe that your first book is a reality. Another beautiful reality about your first book is it's the easiest one to sell. I really didn't have to promote *Blurred Vision* for the first few months (although I still did) because my family, friends, strangers and even enemies supported. People don't always support you because they believe your writing is so great. That may be a hard pill to swallow for some writers but support is support, no matter how it comes.

Whether you're writing a poetry book, novel, cookbook or instructional manual, the feeling of creating and finishing a book is like none other. True, the specifics of the process may be slightly different per genre but seeing your blood, sweat and tears wrapped up in pages and a beautiful cover does something to stir your spirit inside. That time is meant to be savored and enjoyed to the fullest.

One of my best friends says there are two types of writers: "People who are authors and people who happen to write books." Please know that these two types of individuals do not possess the same mentality. The author is the person who aspires to delve into the process, despite the number of peaks and valleys. However, a person who happens to write books is usually in it for a specific end goal: money, clout, recognition, etc.

Can both people exist in one? Of course, but there's usually a skew to one side. Even in those two different mindsets, both types of people deserve to enjoy an accomplishment that many have only dared to dream and neglected to execute: publishing their first (and for some, their only) book.

Regardless of which person you are, a good rule of thumb is announcing your intentions to people you respect and know can hold you accountable. Guard your ideas for your book and don't share them with everyone. There are times that you should share your intentions with people you know have your best interest at heart. Once I started telling people that I planned to write a book, a two-fold reaction began to happen.

First, the people I shared my idea with really began to hold me accountable to my goals and desires. Second, I felt a sense of responsibility that I absolutely had to deliver my book to the masses. I was determined not to be that guy who repeatedly mentioned his "upcoming book" to his close circle and failed to deliver.

Nope.

Remember that to savor the moments of success, those moments must be created first. Once you have your book published, you'll want (and deserve) to celebrate. I once attended a book vendor event and seminar (which was a total waste of money and time, besides the company of great friends) where an author I know spoke before attendees and said authors shouldn't do book signings.

Huh?

I was flabbergasted.

I couldn't believe that he offered that as advice for the hopeful writers (many of which who had just released their first book) at the conference. His thought process was "If it doesn't make money, it doesn't make sense."

Time has a way of revealing things that we often don't believe. Although I felt his delivery was harsh and defeating to new authors, I later came to understand the core of his warning.

Should you have a book signing?

Yes, without a doubt.

How you have the book signing is the more important question you should ask yourself. I went all out for my first book signing, which was held at a swanky sushi restaurant in North Dallas. Despite clearing over $1,000 in sales in just one night (what a time to be alive), my investment to host the book signing totaled over $500. The costs included everything from drinks, food, promotional flyers, balloons, paid social media promotion and a large cardboard banner displayed at the event.

The event was classy and well planned. However, I couldn't help but think how much more profit I could have made if I scaled down my event. In my opinion, it's all about balance. The initial book launch event should be grand to some extent. After all, this is everyone's introduction to a special project you worked on for months or even years in some cases. Once the initial bang has fizzled, it's wise to mix in other vendor events and venues that are low cost. For example, many Half Price Books locations will allow authors to host a two-hour slot for a book signing free of charge. What's the catch? Just proper planning and getting on their calendar in time to host your event. There are countless opportunities that can be leveraged for a successful book launch event.

Some of my most profitable book signings have been held at unconventional venues. Can you imagine a book signing at an ice cream shop? Well, I couldn't either. I had just wrapped up my second novel, *No Cream in the Middle*, in 2017. I was in search of a venue to host a low-cost book launch. Keep in mind, I had released a few books at this point and wanted my book signings to not only make sense but make (many) cents. There was a local ice cream shop that I loved going to in the neighborhood I lived in at the time. I knew I wanted to incorporate some type of dessert in the event. Then it hit me. I went out on a limb and asked the ice cream store owner if I could host my event there.

I recoiled inside as I waited for the answer.

"Yes, of course and we won't charge you anything."

Wait? Was it really that easy? Did I just book a venue for my book launch that I didn't even have to pay for?

Yep.

The book signing brought the ice cream shop more business (from my guests) and I sold more books from strangers that walked in during the event. Don't be afraid to veer from the normal path of hosting a book event, especially if it fits the theme of your book.

Also, when you're scouting out vendor events, don't be afraid to be the only author in the building. In fact, if there are a room full of authors, you may find you have a lesser chance of substantial sales. People will only buy so many books at one time. However, if you're the only author on a row full of vendors selling t-shirts and jewelry, you may have a better chance at profitability.

Picking the right vendor event can sometimes be more profitable than hosting your own event, especially if it's in the same city you've already exhausted. My first few solo events were very well attended because I had many friends and family that supported. Those friends and family told friends and family, which still made future events well attended. Vendor events are great to keep in your back pocket for those lull moments after the initial hype of your book has settled.

Much like you never forget your first, it's great to remember what attracted you to your first. What pushed you to finish writing your book? What moments were you most proud of during the publishing process or when you had the book in hand? Who were the people who were instrumental in your success and spreading the word about your book? Never forget the answers to these questions because they will influence your next best move for your book.

You must often believe the dream even if you don't feel like it's going to come to fruition. It's amazing how people respond to you when you exude a certain level of confidence. This is especially important for first-time authors. I wish I had more of the assured (but not cocky) attitude I have today in regard to my first book. That assuredness makes other people as if they should invest in you because you feel like you're worthy of the investment.

As the old saying goes, 'the first cut is the deepest'. If you're anything like most independent authors, you have several books sitting in your memory banks. The first book is usually the hardest to release because it's unfamiliar territory. After a few tries (and book releases), the process will feel like second nature.

BRAIN PICKERS TO KEEP IN MIND:

- Create an outline for your book.
- Book signings are great, as long as they are strategic and make sense.
- Be unconventional when selling your book.
- Leave room for creative interpretation.
- Remember to smell the roses of your success.

CHAPTER TWO

I Saw the Seventh (7th) Sign

Many first-time authors get asked some of the same questions after their book is released.

"How did you do it?"

It's one thing to get picked up by a publisher and release your first book. Don't get me wrong. That is still a cause for major celebration. However, it's a different ball game when you've had to research all the details, find your own editor, graphic designer (that preferably has experience in designing books) and market with whatever extra money you can spare after all your bills are paid.

Honestly, I don't know how I did it at times. The process for my first book took so long that everything seemed like a blur to me. I didn't start developing a rhythm with my book timelines until around the third release. I was gearing up for my second book, another collection of poetry called *Hindsight 20/20*.

One of my best friends suggested that I start a publishing company. I immediately shot the idea down, thinking it would be too much work. Plus, I didn't want to deal with people in that manner. I can be a handful dealing with myself, let alone another person and the story their packing in tow. Like many other meant-to-be moments in my life, publishing had a way of finding me.

I connected with a coworker at a previous company. She had just published her first book and I noticed she had the name of a publishing company I had never heard of on the spine of her book.

"Nice, who is your publisher? I've never heard of them," I asked naively.

"Let me let you in on a little secret. It's my publishing company," she replied with a mischievous grin.

She had a ton of business sense about her books and publishing. I learned a great deal of the policies I implemented for my own publishing company through her. She believed that people didn't want to hear that her book was self-published so she created her own publishing company.

First, I had to come up with a name. Book titles are one of the most rewarding parts of the book-writing process for me. Once I have the title, the concept for everything else falls in place.

Boom.

That's when it hit me.

7th Sign Publishing.

Seven is one of my favorite numbers for several reasons. There's the biblical reference of it being the number of perfection and completion. I was born exactly seven days after my due date (due on January 28, 1985 and born on February 4, 1985). When I became a member of Alpha Phi Alpha Fraternity, Inc., I was the seventh member to become initiated in my undergraduate chapter. The number seven has always represented great change and confirmation for me. I wanted my publishing company to have that same meaning.

People love the security of a name. Think about it. Would you be so eager to support an unknown author without the backing of a reputable publisher? I'd venture to guess that most people would pass up the book that appeared to be self-published. Although my friend didn't utilize her publishing company to publish books for other authors as I did, it helped her sell her own books. I give credit where credit is due and she hipped me to many things about the independent publishing game.

In the meantime, I gathered as much information as I could about independent publishing houses, self-publishing and traditional publishing. Plus, I had a few real-life experiences to draw from. One of my friends used a publishing house that shall not be named here but they literally locked up access to his book. He was unable to get books printed at a reasonable cost, didn't own the rights to his own work and only received a fraction of the cost.

Publishing has changed over the years and self-published doesn't have to equal poor quality. It's all about the right team of people you have around you to make your book come to life. A top-notch cover designer and a seasoned editor can make all the difference between a professional and unprofessional looking book.

While I researched publishing tips, pitfalls and best practices, I also worked on two books: my second poetry book, *Hindsight 20/20* and *Naked* by John Patrick Adams, which was the first book I published by another author. John was the friend who told me I should start the publishing company. Both books were released within a month of each other and with *Naked*, 7th Sign Publishing was officially off to the races. All those events happened in 2013, a whirlwind of a year that I'll never forget.

The model of 7th Sign Publishing was simple and structured similarly a vanity press (basically a publishing house where authors pay to have their books published). I offered various services to authors, including graphic design, photography (always have a professional headshot on standby), editing, printing, marketing (one of the biggest mistakes I made – we'll get to that later) and more, depending on the author's need. The model catered to indie and first-time authors who needed a one-stop shop to get their books published.

One thing I never did with anyone's book is handled their copyright submission. I guided all of my clients through the process but I wanted them to know I wasn't trying to cheat them. I wanted them to keep the rights to their book. After all, they wrote the words. Seems like that would be a no-brainer, right?

Not necessarily. There are vultures out there waiting to swoop down and devour a great idea from an upcoming author, only to flip it for money or steal the work as their own.

I've always looked out for the best interest of my clients, sometimes to my own detriment. Starting and maintaining a publishing company has been no easy feat. I've even had some people try to steal my "secrets" of publishing to start their own companies – some of which have yet to get off the ground to this day. No one can beat you being you. My customer base was purely word of mouth. People generally took to my personality and genuine transparency, not just the services I provided. As I mentioned earlier, the key is to get people to buy into *you* before your product.

Royalties are also an aspect of publishing I have never explored. As an independent author, it's difficult enough keeping up with my own book sales let alone any else's. Plus, there was no way for me to really know how many books authors sold. The calculation of book sales can become messy when physical copies (I *always* keep books in the trunk of my car) are mixed with Amazon sales (so much so that it has its own chapter) or eBooks. No thanks.

Nonetheless, I was green about the process of meeting with clients compared to how I conduct meetings today. I started thinking of initial client meetings like a math equation. Only five out of ten prospects had a manuscript ready to read. From those five prospects, only three were serious about getting their book to a printed stage. If I was lucky, one out of every ten prospects had a solid manuscript with some form of payment ready to be made shortly after the first meeting.

I used to meet with the same people repeatedly without any compensation (I'm wiser now, thank God). When it comes to publishing (or nearly any business), having a soft spot for a client's story must go out the window. It's all business and no feelings. If a contract is in place, the terms should be followed by both parties and officially amended if both parties agree on any changes to be made. Allowing things to be swept under the rug and then bringing in the legal aspect later only causes more stress for everyone involved.

There have been rare cases when I've met with people who were immediately ready to start the process of getting their book started. Let's say we met in March and they wanted to have their book printed by July of the same year.

Wait.

Can you say, 'No way, Jose'?

Over the years, I've found that it takes most people anywhere from six months to a year or more to get a book to the manuscript stage for editing. Poetry, cookbooks and some self-help books are often exceptions, since they typically don't include as many words as a novel or an educational book.

The editing process alone takes two-three months on the short end.

The graphic design for the cover may also take the same amount of time, depending on the chemistry of the designer and the author.

Yes, chemistry applies to books too. I've worked with many graphic designers for my books (almost a different one for each book). My favorite designers all have one thing in common: they simply get it. There's nothing like a designer that can take a vision and run with it.

Case in point is the cover for my first book, *Blurred Vision*. My original thought was a vision chart like the ones optometrists use. I wanted the title of the book to be mixed in with the chart and have a magnifying glass somewhere on the cover. Sounds simple enough, right? I told the cover designer he could add his own creative input. The cover I chose to print was the one where he still followed the essence of my vision but added his own flare.

Ah, that brings me to another point: the spine. The cover designer must know the exact page count after the book has been edited and formatted to appropriately leave room for the spine of the book. Since this stage is nearly towards the end of the process, cover design is usually the most disjointed aspect of book publishing. For instance, I usually request that the designer creates a front cover for me to start teasing the book on social media, ahead of the release. Then, as everything nears completion, the designer finishes the spine and back cover of the book.

Formatting.

I'll be transparent here and admit I didn't invest in formatting for my first few books. Sure, my margins were set appropriately, and I had a Table of Contents page. After all, that was the bare minimum to be considered legit.

One of my friends gave me a bit of advice on one of my books that I'll never forget.

"Do you mind if I give you a bit of constructive feedback?" he said.

Oh, here we go, I thought.

My defense was already building to combat what he was about to say.

"Sure, what's that?" I responded in a tone that masked my apprehension.

"Your book is great, man. The plot is original but I think the aesthetic inside is lacking a bit. Maybe you can add some chapter heading images in your next book to kick the interior up a notch."

I immediately thanked him for the advice, while simultaneously picking my ego up from the floor.

He was right.

I researched how some of the mainstream novelists' books were formatted and took notes. My next book was sleeker and more modern, thanks to my friend's constructive feedback. Although formatting gave my books a face lift, it also added another two to three months to the publishing timeline.

Then, throw in printing timelines, which can take anywhere from one to two months (especially during major holidays) and you've got yourself a book baby. Nine months is the sweet spot I tell most authors with completed manuscripts. Keep in mind that each aspect of the publishing process has to move like clockwork to make even a nine-month timeline happen.

As I mentioned earlier, many people think there's a magic key that unlocks all the secrets. The truth is there are no secrets. I'm laying it all out here in this book. I don't know it all but I do know what I know. You know how you can have several people cook the same meal using the same recipe and each one tastes differently? Publishing is very similar. No one can be you. Any client that has been for me has been for me. I've turned down working with people before and some people have turned down working with me but there was no love lost. The older I get, the more I see the value in not fighting to prove a point.

If you're looking to start a publishing company, I'd recommend doing extensive research (including reading this book, of course). The concept of a traditional publishing company is swiftly becoming a thing of the past since publishing is so accessible for authors. However, accessibility doesn't equal quality. One of the most important aspects is building a solid team of people. Find a strong editor, graphic designer and formatter (remember the last two are usually two different people). Those three people essentially make up the trifecta of successful independent publishing. Keep in mind these don't have to be people you know. I found my formatter on Reedsy (a wealth of services can be found there). I didn't know him from a can of paint but I loved his portfolio and took a leap of faith. Now, he's my go-to formatter for all my books. He has worked on a few books I published for other authors as well.

Publishing takes commitment. Make no mistake about it. It's one thing to put in blood, sweat and tears towards your own body of work. There's a different level of dedication needed to produce a quality literary work for someone's story with no personal investment. No one wants their vision to be handled haphazardly. When I took on publishing, I was all-in until I decided my time was up.

Since its inception, 7th Sign Publishing has helped authors publish books in several genres including short stories (*Introducing Shirley* by Shirley Thomas) self-help (*How to Win the Dating Game* by John Patrick Adams, *Men = Responsibility* and *Signs: What to Do Whenever You Think You Are Being Cheated On* by J. Gibson), children's books (*Through the Eyes of a Child: Breast Cancer* by Ja Lessa Bonds and *The Champ's Great Fight* by Charolette Washington), Christian devotionals (*The Battle on My Shoulders* by Tiffany James and *I Am the Resurrection* by Reginald Rice), memoirs (*Men Over Me* by Erika Shelton) and finances (*The Single Mother's Path to Wealth* by JaCoi James and *Landlording: The Stepping Stone to Financial Freedom* by Jaran Ramsey).

BRAIN PICKERS TO KEEP IN MIND:

- Build a solid team of an editor, graphic designer and formatter if you decide to start a publishing company (or even if you wish to publish independently as an author).
- Pay attention to who owns your copyright (it should be you).
- Allow for plenty of time to publish your book (nine months is a good sweet spot).
- People love a name. Even if you decide to publish independently, at least register a DBA (Doing Business As) name that represents your book well.
- Independent or self-published should never equal low quality.

CHAPTER THREE

Amazon Is King

You may have remembered that juggernaut retailer named Amazon that I mentioned earlier. Everyone wants their book on Amazon. I get it. Much like the old *Cheers* TV show theme song, we all "want to go where everybody knows your name..." But at what cost?

Amazon's print-on-demand model does have its benefits for saving authors a hefty printing cost. Printing is often the highest cost of producing a book and Amazon eliminates that. However, nothing in life comes free. In exchange for the print-on-demand service, Amazon takes about 35% of each book sale. They also take a percentage to print your book on demand. When it's all said and done, you could be out of as much as 40% for each book sold.

In case you didn't know, your book's ISBN categorizes the format in which your book is sold. If you have a print copy, that's one ISBN (about $85 each). Want to release an eBook as well? That's another ISBN. Thinking about an audio book? You guessed it... another ISBN. Amazon caters to all these book formats and makes it accessible for many authors to publish their own books through Kindle Direct Publishing or ACX.

I like to think of Amazon as exposure. It's a nice-to-have for a validation avenue. I can't tell you how many book vendor events I've been to where people come up to my table (where printed copies are nearly as close to them as white on rice) and ask if my books are available on Amazon. It's a strange phenomenon but many readers won't take an independent author seriously if their book is missing on Amazon.

I've literally had people ask, "Is your book on Amazon?".

If I responded, "No," several of them decided they didn't want to read my book. Imagine that.

Don't get me wrong; many authors have made a mint selling their books exclusively through Amazon or with its online retailers. I'd like to note here that Amazon also has an exclusive eBook program. That means if you decide to sell your eBook there and give them exclusive rights to sell, you can *only* sell it there and not any other online retailer – even your own website. Also, while Amazon does not require you to include a copyright page in your book to publish through them, you should *always* have one.

Amazon has its own special code that can be cracked with careful study and hopping on your big toe ten times while counting to five. I've honestly never invested the time to see how it works. There are specific times of the day and even certain genres that may entice more sales or the chance for a #1 best-seller. Think about a general fiction book that has to climb through such a wide array of other books in its category. Compare that to a book in a Young Adult Sci-Fi category; it's more niche and lends to a greater chance at becoming #1.

I've always favored the perceived harder hustle of selling my books directly or on my own website and receiving all the profit, instead of just a portion. Oh and did I forget to mention that Amazon only pays quarterly? Let's say you sell 100 copies of your book on Amazon the first day of its release. If you retail the book for $15 and Amazon takes an even 40% of each sale, that's $9 per book and a grand total of $900 for the 100 books you sold. Sounds great right? Well, not so much when you have to wait over three months to receive the money. I'd rather have $1,500 instantly for 100 books sold at the $15 price point.

One of the joys of being an independent author is signing your own books. There's nothing like gaining a new reader and signing their book at the point of purchase. Kiss that feeling goodbye if you decide to distribute through Amazon. They tell you how many books you've sold during a given time but not who bought the books. As a result, people can tell you that they've purchased your book on Amazon and you'll never know (unless they show you the book or leave a review).

Reviews are critical to the success of Amazon sales. The more reviews (specifically positive ones), the greater the chance people will notice your book and likely purchase it. If you decide to use Amazon as your primary avenue of selling your book, kindly harass people to leave good reviews for you. In my case, I ask people to leave reviews if they purchase on Amazon. However, my bread and butter comes from my personal website and in-person events. Anything I receive from Amazon or any other online retailer is just icing on the cake.

The printer that I submit my books through offers distribution through Amazon, and Barnes and Noble online for free as a perk to its authors. Amazon also has permission to use the information from your book to place it on other online retailers such as Books-A-Million, Target, Walmart, etc. I've literally had people call and tell me that some of my books had been placed on Target's website. Amazon doesn't provide a schedule of when they will place your book on various retailer sites. They just do it, because they can.

One major benefit that I love about Amazon is the ability to quickly showcase corrected book files. If you notice you've let a few typos slip through in your book, you can submit your file to the printer again (usually for an additional fee). The updated file is typically included in the online version of the book within a few days. That method beats ordering more corrected print copies and waiting two weeks or more for them to arrive.

In a nutshell, I have nothing against Amazon. When I first got my record player in 2020, I received more packages from them in a short time span than I'd like to admit. When it comes to books, I feel like the legwork can be done on the author's side with proper promotion and events. The choice is yours but I choose to utilize Amazon as an additional selling platform, not a primary one.

One way Amazon can truly be beneficial is through eBook and audio book distribution. These are enhancements to your print book. Of course, you can still use Amazon as a print-on-demand distributor. eBooks and audio books have greatly increased in popularity and utilizing online retailers like Amazon to sell in those formats is a smart move. I look at those formats like hoping to win the lottery. It's not wise to quit your day job for a chance at success with the lottery.

True, an author may sell a ton of eBooks or audio books through nonprint formats. Still, that doesn't equal an enormous payout and if it does the author won't see the money immediately. Cash is king and so is print when it comes to instant profits at a higher margin.

Amazon can be an easy way for authors to sell their books at a lower production cost. Again, niche topics and genres tend to do well on Amazon since there are countless books for readers to choose from. If you have a core group of supporters that you know will not only purchase your book on Amazon (and not lie and say they did), plus leave a review, that is the jackpot.

Plus, if you've exhausted inventory of print books, readers can pick up your book from Amazon while the next shipment is being fulfilled (if they just can't stand to wait). To each his or her own, but I purposely mark my books up higher on Amazon. The downside of that is Amazon can change the retail price of your book at will to help increase sales or influence their algorithm. I always push people to my website to purchase books instead of Amazon. After all, your book may be worth a pretty penny one day so the more copies that have your autograph in circulation, the better.

BRAIN PICKERS TO KEEP IN MIND:

- Amazon can be a great way to save on printing costs.
- Reviews. Reviews. Reviews. Ask anyone who purchases your book on Amazon to leave a review.
- Amazon payments are made quarterly, not instantly.
- Amazon takes their cut before you see a penny.
- Place your book in a niche category for a greater chance of visibility and sales.

CHAPTER FOUR

Social Media Is Not Marketing

Remember when Lauryn Hill said, "Respect is just a minimum."? Well, the same thing goes for the use of social media to promote your books. Social media wasn't booming as much as it is now when I released my first book in 2011. As time progressed, it was clear that social media was the necessary first step to marketing and engagement.

It's hard to believe that social media has only been around for about two decades. Facebook launched on my birthday (February 4th) in 2004. Twitter wasn't far behind in 2006 and Instagram in 2010. Needless to say, time has moved quickly and if you want to promote a service or product, social media is a necessity.

I laugh when I hear people say they are taking breaks from social media. Don't get me wrong. I'm not knocking the concept of unplugging from social media. However, as an author and business owner, I don't have that luxury. It takes a few times of people seeing the same thing online before they make a decision. Think about it. Unless it's something you've already had your eyes set on, repeated social media posts, stories and statuses can help sway your decision.

As an author, you *always* have to be on. Shaking hands, kissing babies, accepting friend requests (I'm much more cautious about that now though), you name it. COVID-19 has altered the way we do things in person but it has made the use of social media more critical.

A couple of years ago, I vowed I wouldn't add any other social media platforms besides my Facebook, Instagram and Twitter account. I didn't want to get involved with Snapchat or TikTok. Guess what? Yep, I eventually gave in and activated accounts for both platforms. You never know where someone will notice your work. I've had strangers (some of whom have become friends) on various social media platforms that randomly found my books from a post I made.

Plus, I'd heard of new waves of authors being discovered on TikTok through hashtags like #booktok and #authortok. Whether I wanted to manage another social media platform was beside the point. I wasn't about to potentially lose a chance for exposure on a booming platform.

Some authors or entrepreneurs ponder whether a separate social media account should be created to highlight the specific service he or she is promoting. I prefer to use one account for everything. You get Carlos the poet, publishing consultant, author, music lover and all-around human on one account. However, I do have a specific Facebook page for my books and blogs (Peauxetic Expressions) that is managed separately from my personal page.

Plus, I believe that people often buy into the person and not the product. Although I don't post anything extremely personal on my social media pages, I give enough for people to feel like they know me. Sometimes people take that and run with it, thinking they know you well. However, I'd rather that instead of people only seeing posts about my writing, poetry and books ad nauseum.

With that said, many people (myself included at times) make the mistake of believing that social media is the end-all-be-all when it comes to marketing. Maybe 15 years ago, that was accurate. Now, it's simply the bare minimum. Algorithms make it incredibly hard for your followers to even see what you've posted in today's social media society.

"I posted it on Facebook. Didn't you see it?"

This is something I've heard from many people who post

updates about their products, pictures or even emotional vomiting via a status update.

No, I didn't see it.

Chances are, most of your followers didn't see it either. Think about it. Let's say you have 500 followers. If 70% of them decide to all post on the same day, isn't there a great chance that you may miss many of their posts? The same goes for invites to events through Facebook as well. I remember when I used to utilize Facebook's event creation system and it brought great crowds for my events. That was during the early Facebook days. The same methods don't work as well now.

These days, some of my most successful events (outside of my initial book launches) have been when I partnered with other creatives. We are able to use each other's circle of friends and associates for more exposure. Exposure is the name of the game on social media and any exposure is good exposure. No one wants a nasty scandal or unfavorable attention but sometimes that's exactly what is needed to break through the noise of social media.

Paid advertising through social media can be an effective way to keep your presence top of mind for your followers, people who resemble your followers in activity, or those who fit your target audience. However, paid social media advertising can be a dangerous landmine if you don't know how to properly target a group of people. Plus, it costs to reach the masses. A mere $5, targeting 1,000 people, is only a drop in the bucket for the paid social media arm of your marketing plan. The more individuals you target and the broader your radius, the more money you'll need to back engagement.

Ah, engagement. That elusive word that can't always be measured. Although the golden nugget is getting an online or in-person sale, engagement can come in the form of likes, shares, comments, website clicks and/or even inciting word of mouth. It's easy to become discouraged when funds are spent towards marketing through social media (or other outlets), but people often need to be reminded to decide on a purchase.

Think about those ads that pop up on your news feed that you have fallen prey. Chances are you didn't fall for the ad the very first time it appeared on your timeline. Oh, but it probably got you that second, third or fourth time. Marketing your book is much the same. You have to make people tired of seeing it. They have to think, "Oh here she/he goes promoting that book again." In the words of one of my favorite groups, TLC, the mentality has to be, "Yes, it's me again….and I'm back."

The great aspect about social media is it can bring new audiences and loyal repeat readers. Some of my greatest support has been from strangers I've never met (or met only a handful of times). Those people don't know your biggest fears, your greatest mistakes and all the idiosyncrasies that people who know you might unintentionally use to minimize your work.

My heart goes out to the generation that grew up solely on social media. In my opinion, those individuals have to work harder to ensure they build authentic connections beyond likes, shares and filters. There's nothing wrong with social media and online interactions, but your presence and essence must be felt beyond the phone or computer screen.

I'll never forget an event I participated in back in 2017. I was at a low point financially and I needed to win at that event like never before. Winning was making enough money to pay my rent. I'm proud to say that I did "win" and that event to this day is the biggest single sales day I've ever had at an in-person event. I give credit to God and how he moved through the people to purchase my books.

One lady walked up to my table and questioned everything from the inspiration to the type of paper I printed my books on (literally). I was so annoyed and frustrated near the end of our discussion. By this time, I had spoken with her for over 30 minutes and she hadn't purchased a single book. I'll always remember her next words to me.

How many sales have I missed out on talking to this lady?

I had a hunch that my frustration was beginning to surface on my face.

"Well, it's been great talking to you. I'll get one of each of your books," she uttered calmly.

"Huh? Oh, wait. You want all the books?" I asked, pleasantly surprised.

I was shocked. At that time, I had nine books and she had just committed herself to purchasing every single one of them. That lady not only purchased all my books but she brought other people. They purchased books as well.

That was one of the most joyous days during my journey as an author. Those feelings can't be experienced with online book sales. Sure, videos can be sent via social media channels to express gratitude for a good read. How many times does that happen? Don't worry. I'll wait.

The online presence should only reinforce the physical presence. I've come to learn that authenticity (or at least faking it well) is what makes people pay attention. The term "marketing" is a labyrinth that few have been able to completely figure out. In a fast-paced, short-attention spanned world, interest has to hit and stick quickly.

The impact of marketing is extremely objective, which is why I took it out of my contract after the first few years of publishing. Initially, I promised that I would use my social media platforms to help market books for my clients. However, I soon realized that my efforts were not measurable. Book sales often can't be measured by a single post, tweet or video.

Furthermore, when anyone says they will do marketing for you, the expectation is to *do* marketing for them. The problem with that notion is no one can market you like yourself. I've lost count of how many times I've met a new reader at a vendor event, that person posts my book on their timeline and it gives me exposure to a new group of readers.

Social media may not be marketing but it can definitely give you exposure to circles and groups of people you may not have otherwise made a connection. I met one of my book cover designers through a friend that saw one of my posts about an upcoming book I was working on. She introduced me to the photographer that took my headshots. That photographer in turn introduced me to the cover designer that created two of my book covers. Talk about divine connections.

Marketing (especially via social media) can all be a gamble. However, with a lot of effort, consistency and quality content, it can help place you in proper position. If you don't play, chances of winning are slim.

I once had someone purchase one of my books after I made a five-year anniversary post of a particular book. Even when you think you're posting too much, keep going. If people get sick of seeing you post about your book, keep going. Those people probably won't be the ones to purchase your book anyway.

I'm no expert but I will sprinkle in a few things that I think are bad business when it comes to social media and its close cousin, marketing. One of my biggest pet peeves is when I follow someone on multiple platforms and their content is the same on all platforms. I get it. Many independent authors also hold full-time jobs (including me) and wear many hats.

Sometimes I don't follow the trends of the best times to post based on my platform engagement (remember, I work a full-time job outside of this). In fact, most of my posts are made during my morning workouts. The stair master is where it usually happens. Wherever you can fit it in – do it. Create consistency but keep in mind that variety is the spice of life. The latter can also be said regarding differentiating posts on your social media platforms.

Each post should make sense. Follow certain hashtags that pertain to your business. Make sure your camera lens is clean when you take photos. I know it sounds elementary but I'm guilty of it all the time. Apps like Canva offer pro versions at an affordable monthly subscription (less than a fast-food drive-thru combo meal). You can create business cards, flyers, social media stories and posts. Also, Fiverr is a great resource if you just want to send someone a flyer concept and allow them to create one for you. Reedsy is an excellent resource as well if you're looking for a great cover designer, editor, formatter and more. Just be prepared to spend a little more on the latter platform. However, I can attest that the money there is well spent.

Tie in social media through every way you can to support your marketing efforts. I wrapped up two podcasts in 2022, one of which accompanied my novel, *Trigger Pointe*. That podcast talked about life's moments that trigger us. The other podcast, Brown Liquor and Cigars, was one I did with my friend, John, where we talked about love and relationships from a male's perspective.

Although the latter podcast had nothing to do with my writing directly, we shared the episodes every week on social media for three years before we decided to call it quits. Many of the show's listeners supported my books through getting to know me on the podcast. I was the "it depends" or the "chill" one of the group, minus a few topics we discussed where I had heated opinions. They also came to know me as an author.

I had the courage to create my third and latest podcast, The Water Bearer Podcast (ironically inspired by one of the last Brown Liquor and Cigars episodes) about dealing with an Aquarius (my Zodiac sign) and interactions with the entire zodiac sphere. The experience from the previous podcasts sparked the idea for yet another direct, creative avenue for me to express myself and an indirect avenue to continue to promote my writing.

While we're on the podcast topic, it's not all about the best microphone or soundboard. Don't get me wrong. You want your presentation to be of good quality. After all, you want to put your best foot forward. However, there are several programs like StreamYard that allow you to broadcast video podcasts and then share them on social media.

Many opportunities mean more than meets the eye. It's about seizing the moment and letting your light shine for people to get to know you… and hopefully buy your product. You are the product and your book is the byproduct of your creative genius.

BRAIN PICKERS TO KEEP IN MIND:

- Social media posts are not enough for your marketing plan. It's just the basics.
- Look beyond your friends and family for support.
- Think of unique ways like podcasts and other unconventional avenues to promote your book.
- Investigate sites like Reedsy, Fiverr and Canva for marketing and publishing resources.
- Pay attention to when your followers are most engaged with your content.

CHAPTER FIVE

Keep Your Friends Close and Enemies Closer

When it comes to being an independent author, the old saying, "Keep your friends close and your enemies closer," couldn't be truer. I have been blessed to have some amazing friends that have supported not one but several (in some cases, all) of my books. However, I realize the rarity of that support. I also have seen the other side of the coin where strangers have been some of my biggest supporters.

It sounds counterintuitive that friends often don't support as well as people who have lack a vested interest in us. I believe that's just the thing. The vested interest our friends have in us sometimes minimizes our efforts. Before you go crossing off people on your friend list, hear me out. I don't believe that friends and even family deliberately mean to miss the bar on support. Nonetheless, the people that love us the most can often put us in a box.

I've had some friends and family say things to me like, "Oh are you still writing books?"

Of course, on the surface, that seems like a valid question. The question comes across as sketchy when people just liked a post about your book earlier that day.

The nerve.

I digress.

Over time, I accepted that everyone has so many things going on in their personal lives that my latest book release is often not top of mind. I used to feel slighted because I'm the friend that supports if one of my friends starts a business or launches a new product.

In times like these it's best to take a page from *The Four Agreements* by Don Miguel Ruiz, one of the most influential books I've ever read. One of the book's four core principles is to not take things personally. The principle is simple yet true. The quicker that truth can be embraced as an author, the thicker your skin will become. In fact, avoiding taking things personally is a great way to live life in general.

Friends and family will often support your first two or three books because the feeling is fresh. However, those same friends and family may easily become exhausted with supporting you after book number three. I experienced some of that right before I released my first novel, *Fortune Cookie*. Besides *Blurred Vision*, *Fortune Cookie* is the second most important book in my catalog. It introduced me to a new audience of novel readers and people who may not be fans of poetry. As I mentioned earlier, poetry is often a love-it or hate-it type of genre.

The novel introduced me to a new audience and reignited interest from people close to me. Many of the strangers I gained as readers for my first novel picked up my old books and have continued to support my other books released afterwards. Strangers will often be a mouthpiece for your book and give genuine feedback. If they love it, they will tell their friends who in turn will support you as well.

One time I ran into a lady I met at a poetry event I participated in while I was checking out at Walmart. This had been since the COVID-19 pandemic and masks made it hard to recognize her.

However, she recognized me and said, "Hey, aren't you a writer?"

"Yes, I am," I responded, surprised that she was even able to recognize me with a mask.

She then went on to tell me how much she enjoyed the books that she purchased from me.

I wasn't having the best day then and I thanked her immensely for such a gracious compliment. She had no idea how much her unexpected expression of her enjoyment of my books impacted me.

Those types of experiences are always exceptionally special when they come from strangers. There's a certain conviction that a stranger has that admires your work over someone who knows us. Don't get me wrong. Support is support and it should be received however it is given. Nonetheless, the average person minimizes a co-sign of a family member or friend. The notion is that person is supporting to be nice because it's someone they love.

Here's another concept that may seem strange but it works. Tell your enemies about your book as well. There's a certain curiosity that enemies have that draws them to us. They don't want anything to do with us but enemies are often willing to support monetarily to satisfy their curiosity.

Let them.

I've had people purchase my books that I know beyond a shadow of a doubt despise me. I questioned it at first until I realized a sale is a sale. The worst that could happen is they use the book as a coaster. The best that could happen is they read it and spread the word.

There's nothing quite like word of mouth. It can spread like wildfire now, especially with avenues like social media. Impact and influence help readers see and pay attention to your book. Those "readers" may be individuals that don't even purchase books at all. There are countless reasons why people buy books, including, of course, being an avid reader of a certain genre, needing a distraction from something in their life, as a gift or maybe motivation to embark upon a new habit in their life. Either way, we want to be front and center as independent authors when those people are ready for a new literary treasure.

Let's get back to these enemies for a second. There are some who qualify as enemies within a peer group. Imagine independent authors being enemies of each other. It happens. I've had other authors try to compete with me and even seen future books they released that resembled concepts of my previous releases.

It's all par for the course. I like to stay on my toes and ahead of what the next person is thinking. The independent publishing world is smaller than it looks. Readers can tell who came up with ideas on their own and who didn't. The best attitude to have is to stay original and follow your gut.

No one can beat you being you. I personally don't like to watch much TV when I'm writing a fiction novel. You'd be surprised how entertainment on TV can seep into your own creativity. I prefer for my ideas to be own, as much as possible. Nothing is totally new under the sun but I pride myself on highlighting original elements in all of my novels.

Silence the noise and the haters to reach your goals. When you're done, use those same haters to be the mouthpiece for your marketing efforts. They're already paying attention to what you're doing anyway. Why not use them for a good cause? One way to tell if people don't really mean you well but are interested in your projects is if they never congratulate you.

How easy is it to give a love, like or leave a congratulatory comment on a post? Those same lurkers will often watch every story you post on social media but rarely support. Believe me when I say more people are watching than you believe. Give them something to talk about. Give them a show every time they come across your social media page. Chances are they will slip up and promote your work, even if that isn't their intention.

It took me a few years to learn that the best approach for every book I write is to promote it like no one knows me. After all, if some of your biggest supporters will be strangers, the pitch has to be enticing. What will make them pick up (or download) your book over anyone else's? The market is extremely flooded with books so it's critical now more than ever to stand out.

Ask yourself how you would describe your book to a potential reader in 30 seconds or less. Could you tweet it in a concise manner that grabs the reader's attention? I'll be the first to admit, I can be a little longwinded (I guess that's why I'm a writer). However, when it comes to marketing a book, authors must cut to the chase quickly.

Here's an example. My first novel, *Fortune Cookie*, is about a deadly secret between two sisters that gets revealed. There's just enough to get the gist of the story without spilling an immense number of details. Nothing is an absolute when it comes to what will attract readers. Yet, we want to make the story as enticing as possible.

This is where an enemy or "frenemy" can really help promote your work. Never rule these types of people out in your marketing strategy. Someone who doesn't think too highly of you will avoid sharing elaborate details about your book. They will automatically be concise and streamlined when they speak about your book because they don't want to talk about you too long anyway. Use that energy to your advantage.

BRAIN PICKERS TO KEEP IN MIND:

- Family and friends mean well but they can sometimes minimize your work because they know you.
- Switch it up with different genres or writing styles to keep the interest fresh for your readers.
- Don't exhaust your core group of supporters. Target people you've never met as well.
- Practice describing your book to others in less than 30 seconds.
- Use your enemies to spread the word about your work.

CHAPTER SIX

All Clients Are Not Created Equally

I really underestimated the time and effort it would take to become a publisher ten years ago. I knew there would be some sweat equity involved but I wasn't prepared for the various personality differences, setbacks, and financial roadblocks to get to the final published book.

Don't get me wrong. The past ten years have been extremely rewarding, which includes helping authors get their books published for the masses. In the beginning, I was somewhat naïve about contracts and sticking to my guns. If I had a stronger grip on that part and set certain boundaries, my patience wouldn't have waned as thin over the last few years.

My mother was so helpful in getting my contracts solidified. I remember we discussed many different scenarios that could have happened. We pretty much covered every scenario. As fate would have it, a few slight things had to be amended but only years down the line. I'll get to those legal loopholes in a bit. I also consulted some legal professionals I knew to ensure all my contractual line items were above board and fair.

When I first launched my publishing company, I allowed my heart to lead many of my decisions. Unfortunately, hearts and business don't mix well. I met with some individuals several times for free. If I was lucky, I may have gotten a meal or two. In some instances, I even drove on the other side of town to meet these people. Looking back on it, I was not good at setting boundaries.

Independent publishing can be rewarding but it can also be very taxing when you have a full-time job. There were many days I would get off work around 6:00PM and then drive straight to a potential client for a meeting. Many of those meetings went nowhere for various reasons. Some people weren't serious about publishing a book and only wanted to brainstorm ideas. Some people didn't have the money to move forward. Then, there were others who got cold feet about sharing their story with the masses.

The first book I published really spoiled me. John, whom I mentioned earlier, took a chance and published his first book, *Naked*, with 7th Sign Publishing. It was a huge gamble for him. I was transparent with him that I was learning along the way. I'm always indebted to him for being the first author outside of myself to kick off my publishing company. He even published his second book, *How to Win the Dating Game*, through me as well. Both books were a great success for him.

"This publishing thing is a piece of cake," I told myself.

Little did I know the ride I was in for after the first year I launched my publishing company. My second client, Shirley Thompson, was fairly easy too. She had a collection of short stories, which I loved. Within my first two books published, I covered two different genres – self-help and fiction. My motto was I would publish all genres except for anything demonic, extremely risqué or highly educational (similar to a classroom textbook).

Shirley's book was a lesson for me about the importance of an image and how different opinions can form about something as simple (yet extremely important) as a book cover. We reviewed several book cover samples and the one she eventually chose was a close-up shot of a lady's face. The lady was clearly African American in the photo. Back then, it wasn't quite as popular to have a brown face on a book cover as it is now. I know, it sounds crazy considering that was almost ten years ago.

Shirley was conflicted because some people loved her cover and others thought that she limited her audience by featuring a brown face. I've always tried to remain as neutral as possible with faces on my book covers. Nonetheless, this was her book and I only wanted to offer suggestions instead of demands. Eventually, she settled into the decision for her cover and was proud of her book.

Fast forward: I published a second book for Shirley, *Hidden Love*, right before I ended 7th Sign Publishing as an avenue for independent authors to publish their books. I was elated and grateful that after all that time since her first book, she thought of me to publish her second one.

Around the same time when I published Shirley's first book, I started working on two other relationship and self-help themed books by J. Gibson, *Men = Responsibility* and *Signs*. Working with J. Gibson was a reminder that we must never underestimate the power of mutual connections. J. Gibson and I share mutual friends and we would always see each other at our friends' Halloween party each year. Eventually, J. Gibson reached out to me and let me know he was working on publishing two books.

Soon after working with him, the publishing process became somewhat sporadic and a little less busy in terms of actual books I published. There were spurts here and there, including a touching children's book I published for a friend and former coworker, *The Champ's Great Fight* by Charolette Washington, about her son's fight with cancer, and *The Single Mother's Path to Wealth* by JaCoi James.

I barely even had the opportunity to meet JaCoi. We connected by chance at a vendor event that I decided to participate in at the last minute. The event was somewhat of a dud before I met her. Vendor events can really be tricky. Often times, the vendor table may be anywhere from $50 to $200, during an average of a four-hour span. Some events don't have the foot traffic they promote and if they do, some people simply don't wish to spend their money on books. That day, I was barely able to break even and I was a bit disgusted.

JaCoi walked up to me literally as I was breaking down my table. We exchanged information and she expressed that she was very serious about starting her book to use as an accompanying tool for her consulting business. Although I heard similar declarations before, something seemed different about JaCoi. I loved her tenacity and business sense. She knew what she wanted and that made her a pleasure to have as a client. Right before I started working with her, I contemplated ending 7th Sign Publishing. After all, I had completed the mission I set out to do by then.

I helped several authors publish their books and released a few more books of my own during that time. Nonetheless, I decided to refrain from throwing in the towel. I grew weary of talking to so many people that fell through with starting their book with me. Ironically, it wasn't a shot at my ego whenever an author decided not to publish with me.

My thought was always, "How can I get back all this time I wasted?"

Time is money and I've learned that it cannot be wasted in any facet of life, let alone publishing a book. Everything happens for a reason. I don't necessarily believe it is wasted time if a lesson can be learned. However, I wish I had learned some of the lessons in reclaiming my time a bit sooner than I did!

As with any business, all customers are not pleasant to work with. One person who I won't name made me so angry, I was ready to fight...literally. The way he handled business was so ignorant. There were red flags that let me know it might not be a great business partnership from the very beginning.

He and I went back and forth on the final amount that would be charged for his book. He basically wanted me to reduce my price by nearly $1,000 and still receive the same level of service.

Excuse me?

Never diminish your value for anyone or anything, even if you're in dire need of business. Sometimes it's best to hustle another way or just be broke if it means you have to lower your standards to do business with some people. Although I didn't work with that client (who I confidently say was my most difficult client ever) for money, I should have been more solid in my boundaries. As I mentioned earlier, editing is a source of contention for many author and publisher relationships. My client threw me for a loop when he said he didn't want the edited version of his book to be published. He claimed he already edited the book himself.

Excuse me? I thought again.

This could not be real.

I reluctantly agreed to publish his book as is, only if I removed the 7th Sign Publishing branding. After all, I wasn't about to let him mess up the name I worked so hard to build. A few weeks before his book was set to go to print, he came back with many "errors" he wanted to correct in the book. Keep in mind these same "errors" were originally corrected in the first round of editing.

After the horrible experience with him, I knew my passion for publishing was waning. Oh and I'd be remiss to mention that the same client tried to get me to sign a document relinquishing my rights as his publisher over a year after we agreed to that very thing (right before I submitted this book for editing). I say we "agreed" because of an email I sent that stated no response by a certain date equaled consent.

Yep. You guessed it.

The deadline passed and I moved forward with removing his book from online circulation, as he originally requested.

Literally right before the pandemic hit, I met a real estate agent named Jay Ramsey. He purchased one of my books at a vendor event I participated in the weekend before the world went on lockdown. He also mentioned he was looking for a publisher for his first book. We exchanged contact information, but I really didn't put much stock in our dialogue. Remember, I had just come off a nightmare of a client situation.

A few days later, Jay reached out to me in response to an

email I sent inquiring about his book. I always make sure I do my due diligence and follow-up with any prospects, regardless of whether I think it will pan out to be an active client. Jay was surprisingly ready to go. He had a vision, title ideas, charts that he wanted to include in the book and a working draft that was nearly completed.

Jay made his first payment and I was off to getting his book to the finished stage. I contracted out all the work for the book so I didn't get my cut until towards the end of the process. The editor, graphic designer, photographer and interior designer all got their money first before I saw a penny. That was how I conducted the business for all my books.

The book launch for Jay was rushed but very successful for him. We rushed to get that book out by the first of the year (his preferred release date). I was extremely anxious because he had already set a book signing which I cautioned against until we had physical books in hand. He was proof that with a supportive base of people, a profitable book launch is more than attainable.

Not only did the books arrive just in the nick of time, but he made so much money from presales that he nearly paid for his cost of publishing the book.

That's how you do it.

Jay challenged me in ways that no other client had before. It was honestly what I needed especially since 7th Sign Publishing as I knew it was about to close its doors for business.

One of the most frustrating things about having books available for my authors on online retailer sites was dispersing funds. It was like I was an accountant for many people, including myself. The more clients I added to my roster, the more taxing it became. The printing company I use only had a bank account setup for one person per account at the time. I would send sales reports monthly to clients that sold books in that timeframe with payment to follow as soon as it hit my account.

As you can imagine, that process left room for doubt at times with some of my clients, especially Jay. He asked several valid questions that I had been working on but honestly didn't have the time to resolve.

"How do I know all the sales are accurate?"

"What happens if God forbid, you die or you're inaccessible?

"How do I get my payments?" he asked.

These were legitimate questions that lit a fire under me as a business owner. Never get too complacent that you fail to learn from other people, even if it's a client. By the time I worked with Jay, I knew the steps to publish a book with my eyes closed but he pushed me to another level. With some constant hounding towards my printer and research, I found a loophole to make it happen.

Now, not only was Jay able to get his book payments from Amazon and other online retailers directly, but I slowly implemented the same setup for all my legacy clients as well. You had to be there to understand how relieved and accomplished I felt to satisfy a client's demand and one of my own simultaneously.

While I was in the process of transferring the setup for my clients, one of my prior clients reached out and told me she wanted her book taken out of circulation.

Huh?

I really couldn't believe what I heard.

She proceeded to tell me that she felt like the book wasn't a good representation of who she was. The author, who I won't name here, had become a minister since she wrote many of the poems in her book.

I came up with an idea for her to have a good-vs-evil type of book that included poems of the woman she used to be and the woman she was currently. The idea was unique in my mind and something that I hadn't seen before in a poetry book. However, she didn't want to promote a book that reminisced on her "sinful" life. I understood but I thought the timing was just unfortunate for her. She paid money and spent time fulfilling her dream.

Suddenly, all of that seemed like it was in vain and gone overnight. Nonetheless, I had to avoid injecting my feelings in the situation. She ultimately didn't want the book in circulation and I removed it as she wished.

Conversely, one of the best client experiences I had was with Erika Shelton. I met Erika through our mutual friend, Tammie, who is more like a sister to me, and we initially started a book process that was halted a while before we started again. When Erika was ready the second time, she was truly ready. By then, she had also launched her own lipstick line and gained a following.

Erika's book was personal to her and detailed her relationships with various men in her life, including her father. I expected her to get cold feet about releasing the book at some point but she never did. She stood firmly in her truth and I respected her for that.

Ja Lessa Bonds was yet another great client I published. Her book, *Through the Eyes of a Child: Breast Cancer*, was a heart-warming children's book that gently addressed reality for children that may lose loved ones to cancer. I believe that no meeting or connection is accidental. Ja Lessa proved that because I used to work with her mother at Frito Lay. Her mother referred her to me and the rest is history.

Closing the door to publishing for other authors has always been delayed for me. There are several people I've spoken with that I promised I would publish books for (likely under their own moniker if it happens) before I decided to put 7th Sign Publishing to bed.

Kandice Wade was not only one of my last publishing clients but my first consulting client. My goal was to launch 7th Sign Consulting LLC around the time of this book's release.

God had other plans.

I've known Kandice for about 15 years since our days of working at Countrywide Home Loans together. She was always professional, warm-spirited and fun to be around. We met through our mutual friend (and my fraternity brother) Adrian Brown, who is now deceased.

Life is unpredictable. I never thought I'd be writing this without Adrian seeing this book come to fruition. I mentioned that I was writing it before he passed and he was excited for me. We didn't talk every day but he was always dependable, provided a good laugh and consistently supported my books over the years.

He and Kandice came to a book signing and wine tasting I hosted in 2019. Suddenly, it was a Countrywide Home Loans reunion. Adrian worked there too and he was responsible for getting me a promotion. I stayed long enough for him to get his bonus (barely three months) before I decided I couldn't take it anymore. We laughed about those early professional days in our career. Kandice and I continued to casually chat since that meeting.

She eventually revealed that she had been battling multiple sclerosis and wanted to write a book about her experience.

I was shocked.

Kandice never complained about anything. I naively assumed everything was great in her life. She hid her pain and documented her story in the process. My respect for her grew even more because of her tenacity.

She soon told me she wanted to release her book. She had a concept, title and direction she wanted to take for marketing as well.

There was one problem.

I told her I was about to stop publishing for other authors.

She understood and what she uttered next shocked me.

"Ok, well how I about I be your first consulting client? You can help me publish my book too and I'll release it under my own company name."

Hmmmm. She presented a solid case.

It was the perfect setup for me to get my feet wet in consulting and help her publish her book without the 7th Sign Publishing label.

I agreed and we worked feverishly on getting her book published. The process felt so much smoother than before, not only because Kandice was easy to work with but because I didn't carry the weight of being the publisher.

Although 7th Sign Publishing as I knew it was closing after nearly ten years, I had no regrets. I felt like I was going out like a champ, starting the next chapter while closing another one. I felt convicted that I made the right decision. I was still poised to help authors publish their books but on more manageable terms.

BRAIN PICKERS TO KEEP IN MIND:

- Meet people where they are but be smart about it.
- Your time is valuable. Don't be afraid to make people pay for it.
- Let your instinct determine when it's time to move forward or call it quits.
- Thorough contracts will help you sleep better at night.
- You're never too seasoned in your craft to learn something new.

CHAPTER SEVEN

Now It's Getting Serious

One of the best traits an author, artist or creative person can have is recognizing when growth is necessary. Although I had found success with publishing for ten years, I began to feel like something was still missing. There was still another level that I needed to reach.

Ever since I was a kid, I enjoyed going left when everyone else went right. I love being different, no matter how anxious it may make me at times. There's a price to pay for being different. During my publishing and author journey, one of those shining moments for me is when I utilized Kickstarter, a crowd funding site, to fund *Fortune Cookie*, my first novel that I mentioned earlier.

I researched the inner workings of how I could try something different for my new novel. As I mentioned before, it's always a great idea to find out how you can reinvent yourself over time. Plus, I was about to get married around that same time. I had the money to pay for the book out of pocket but weddings are expensive. Oh, and did I say weddings are expensive? Crowd-funding my novel seemed like the best route to go to be cost effective and creative at the same time.

People within my close circle gave me feedback about the Kickstarter, mostly positive and some cautionary. My ultimate decision was to move forward with the campaign and I was so glad I did. I asked for $1,000 and made nearly twice that amount.

Kickstarter is all or nothing so I gritted my teeth until I hit my goal. If I made $999, I would have lost all the pledges I received. Whew.

Thank God I made it. I did another Kickstarter for *Stingrays*, a poetry book that I released, a couple of years later. That campaign also proved to be successful. Once again, I surpassed my goal.

The entire time I ran my publishing company, I thought about getting an LLC but really didn't see where it would be beneficial. I saved all my receipts for tax purposes and only hired people on a contractual basis. I used editors, graphic designers, interior designers and photographers by project. The process was seamless and I never had any issues. However, there is a time for evolution in everything.

Now that 7th Sign Publishing is entering a new, consulting phase, I feel that it's time for me to move forward as an LLC. Even more important than that is trademarking my social media handle, Peauxetic. That name is also part of my website, Peauxetic Expressions.

I pride myself in being unique. When I first thought of the name "peauxetic" (pronounced "poetic") over ten years ago, I knew it would be a name that most people (and hopefully no one) would have. At that time the "oh" sound replaced with "eaux" wasn't used too often unless the business or person had Louisiana roots, which I have.

Now, it's everywhere. People use it as slang now and even in popular culture. Take Jazmine Sullivan's Grammy Award winning album, *Heaux Tales*. The substitution is now mainstream. Imitation is supposedly the best form of flattery but I've seen three separate instances where someone has used Peauxetic in their social media handle. I felt more frustrated than flattered.

As a result, I decided I would move forward in trademarking my social media handle. I was taken aback when I realized the "Peauxetic" username had already been taken when I set up my TikTok account. At that point I started looking into the trademark first. Although the LLC was important, the trademark for my name felt like more of an immediate action. However, I found out that the LLC is an umbrella of sorts that covers the trademark. So, I had to shift my attention to establishing the LLC first. It cost me several hundred dollars but it was well worth the investment. In my younger years, I would have gawked at paying money for a trademark (and LLC) for a name I came up with for free. That was before I understood the power of a name and branding.

I'll never forget seeing the Tina Turner movie, *What's Love Got To Do With It*, when I was a kid. There's a scene where Tina Turner (played by the incomparable Angela Bassett) is in court during the divorce proceedings with Ike Turner (played by Laurence Fishburne).

She told the judge, "He can take everything but I get to keep my name. I worked too hard for it."

Oh, poor Tina.

Who the heck would pass up money for a name?

Little did I know her move was well played. Ike knew it too because he became irate that she wanted to keep the Tina Turner name.

I didn't understand it all then but I do now.

People started to know me as "Peauxetic" over the years from my social media platforms. I even performed spoken word at open mics sometimes under that name.

A name is sometimes all you have in business. It's what people come to know before they meet you in person or if they ever meet you in person at all. I love coming up with names and concepts for my book or anything creative. When I stopped publishing for other authors, that was immediately one of the things I missed. Several of the authors I worked with didn't already have titles for their book (which I preferred). That gave me a chance to offer suggestions and some of those titles I threw out ended up becoming some of their final book titles.

Besides next-level business add-ons like an LLC or trademark, there are several things you can do to sharpen your craft that don't require as much money. There are countless YouTube videos, online courses and seminars available to help authors gain the most from their business. I am often baffled at how far resources have advanced since publishing my first book to now.

Also, if you have the luxury of not being tied to a full-time job (although some may argue it's more difficult without steady income), there should be plenty of time to plan, prepare and execute. Those three actions will take you further than you can imagine. As I alluded to earlier, being an author is not about your feelings; it's about making your story enticing for readers.

Rome wasn't built in a day and neither is your writing career. Actually, let's take a step back. Remember there are two types of authors: those who enjoy writing and those who just happen to have written a book. Know which one you are, then go forth on that platform. The latter is just someone who publishes a book with no end goal or solid expectations. There is nothing wrong with this type of person. However, if you identify as the former, you have to roll up your sleeves and invest in yourself.

The average cost of an independently published book can be anywhere from $2,000 to $10,000 (or more). Money has to be spent wisely and it's always a great idea to spend it in a calculated as opposed to a frivolous manner. I remember spending money on bookmarks for a book release that ultimately weren't worth the investment. Sure, they looked nice. People "oohed" and "awed" over them, perhaps to build up my ego. Nonetheless, in today's digital world, tangible products aren't always what your audience wants.

Since printing is the largest cost for most authors to publish a book, some people opt for releasing their book in formats like an audio book or eBook instead. The caution I would give is if you are truly doing it because that's where most of your readers will be, go for it. However, if most of your readers plan to support you with a physical copy of your book, you don't want to cut that corner. Sometimes limited-edition runs or alternate covers may help increase urgency with readers to make your cost back. Set a limited print run during your book launch and let your supporters know that after those copies run out, they can only purchase through online services like Amazon or Audible. You'll get more sales quicker and make a return on your initial investment faster.

Although independent publishing can feel like a revolving financial door, it can be easier to reach a profitability point because royalties don't have to be paid. You are the royalty. Isn't that awesome? Of course, that route takes more elbow grease but I have always favored the independent route. Honestly, I'm not sure if I would ever want to have a traditional publishing deal.

Traditional publishers often don't put in the work that you would render independently because they are not as invested (and rightfully so). Their main objective is to make money and get their investment back. The closest thing I would want to a traditional publishing deal would be to have a reputation as the Chance the Rapper of books. In case you haven't heard of him, he's an independent rapper that has made it mainstream, selling (and making) millions on his own terms. That's success in my eyes.

There are things you can do as an independent or aspiring author today to set yourself up for success. I'm no accountant or tax expert by any means. However, there are a few things that can be done to ensure a return on your investment for your book. For instance, saving receipts can be a life saver. Meals, dry cleaning, gas and even internet usage can be used to help offset your business cost. Again, I don't prepare taxes but I do know a thing or two about using what you have to get the most out of your resources.

If you have chosen to be an author (and not someone who just writes books for fun), many everyday tasks should be viewed through the lens of a business. This doesn't mean that we become robotic in our approach to dealing with people or making decisions. However, it does mean that we realize the value of time and money. The more we respect that relationship, the easier things become. I wish I fully understood that concept when I was younger. Hear it from me now and don't let experience be your teacher.

I'm a firm believer that hard work often beats talent. Some of the most successful people are at a certain level not because their talent is so great but because they worked harder than everyone else. I don't necessarily subscribe to the idea that people should "sleep when their dead" or believe that "sleep is overrated". Make no mistake, your body has a way of letting you know when you're doing too much. Personally, I am just coming out of (and by that I mean, more days than not) the vicious cycle of work, work, work, crash and burn and then do it all over again. Your body has to have time to heal and relax.

Also, an author, there has to be time allowed for us to breathe in life. Take in the negatives, positives, wins, losses, disappointments, heartbreaks, and everything that makes us feel. As I look back on some of the most painful moments of my life, I can see how I was able to channel that energy into my writing. Had I not had those experiences, I know without a doubt that my writing would have lacked certain elements of character. I don't enjoy setbacks or heartaches, just like the next person. I've just become more aware of how I can redirect that energy into my work that will hopefully inspire someone else.

BRAIN PICKERS TO KEEP IN MIND:

- Invest in yourself like your life depends on it.
- Solidify your brand before someone else uses your brand to solidify their brand.
- Try different strategies for your book rollouts to gain maximum exposure.
- Be willing to work harder (and smarter) than the next person.
- Rest is critical for a renewed mind and creativity.

CHAPTER EIGHT

Find Your Joy!

Alright, I hope that if you've made it this far in the book, you have the tools and assurance to start brainstorming, complete your first book or start your second book. There's so much an author has to remember, including outlines, first drafts (maybe second, third and fourth drafts), editing, cover designs, photography for promo, marketing, social media, copywriting, etc. Geesh! All of it can be a headache.

True, there are commitments and deadlines that must be taken seriously. After all, the labor of months or even years of work is being presented to all the masses to consume and unfortunately, critique. However, there has to be room for fun as well. Take time to smell the roses and recognize each accomplishment along the way.

Several people close to me have told me that I don't know how to relax. So, this chapter more than any of the others speaks to the choir. Part of the reason why I've been able to write so many books is because the people close to me likely have a good point. I'm always thinking and creating. My mind never stops. Over the years, I have said that I was taking a break from writing for a bit. My mind would always win because I'd think of an idea for the next book shortly after I made that statement.

Now, I just roll with the ideas as they come. I wish I had more of that carefree spirit when I first started writing. The same passion that drives me to write is the same passion I should have had to celebrate myself.

"But I've only written one page this week."

"I'm only at the brainstorming stage of my book."

"My book title has come to me but not the structure of the book."

So what?

There is a win within all these statements. The problem is we often allow ourselves to be so critical that we miss the milestones, whether large or small.

Celebrate all the moments that brought you where you are today. If you're blessed enough to have people in your life that support you, they will celebrate you. An awareness and sense of self will carry you even further during those doubtful times when you're writing alone.

I remember my first book launch very well but not so much about how I felt. It was all a blur. I remember nearly everyone that came out to support. However, I wish I recalled more of the euphoric feeling of having physical copies of my book to sell.

The whole experience was sensory overload.

Guests.

Food.

Cash for change.

Drinks and drink tickets.

A fancy pen. Every author needs a well-working and eye-catching pen for autographs.

Promo materials.

Cake. Ok, this one isn't a necessity. Nonetheless, it's a celebration. What better way to celebrate than eat cake?

Much like that piece of cake we eat at parties and weddings, we have to remind ourselves to take a slice of joy in between the hustle and bustle.

I've heard many people say that their goal as an author is to win an award, sell a million copies or get rich. Don't get me wrong. All those things can be excellent icing on top of your 'cake' (goal) of being an author. Awards and money should never be the driving force to push anyone to write, in my opinion.

The recognition will keep you afloat for a little while. The passion will keep you in the race long after everyone else has chosen to bow out. Find your 'why' (reason) and let that propel you forward. The process of writing a book can be grueling. Pick out the tasks you look forward to most when preparing your book release.

I love book titles and thinking of book cover ideas. I can't design a book cover to save my life, but I can at least give guidance to an artist for my vision. Those are the aspects of the book process that I enjoy. Have a vision or moment that makes you remember your 'why' as you move along through the journey of publishing and/or marketing your book.

Energy is a funny thing. People can sense when we don't believe in what we're telling them. Conviction can even sell a horrible story. I've been there before and supported products that I didn't like or wouldn't use only because the seller was so enthusiastic. Their energy was infectious, and it made me believe I had to have what they were selling. That kind of energy is what you need to sell anything. After all, people ultimately buy into the person over the product.

I know what you're thinking.

"I'm not happy every day."

Yes, I get it and to that I say, "Neither am I."

Life is more than just a feeling. It's an action. One of my former pastors, Dr. Lynn Murray, used to always render a quote that stuck with me as a little boy through current day as a grown man.

"You just keep doing the right act and the right attitude will follow."

A little light flickered in my brain. I didn't fully understand the depth of his statement but life taught me a few experiences along the way that made me say, "Ah, yes. I get it now."

Much like it takes multiple times for an idea or marketing

tactic to stick with an audience, it's the same for finding the joy in your process as a writer. Don't be afraid to push yourself but also know your limitations. I may set a goal of writing five to seven pages in a week for a book. A single mother of two children with a full time job may not be able to commit to the same goal. Nonetheless, set an achievable goal, stick to it and celebrate each time you do *anything* to work towards accomplishing that goal.

If you're doing an interview or podcast, let people see and feel your energy. I've listened to several authors before give unenthused accounts of their books. Unfortunately, that didn't entice me to purchase their book even if it had a great story line.

I get it.

I'm mostly a laid-back guy. So, I have to step outside of my comfort zone at times to demonstrate my excitement about projects. If not, everything just comes across as way too "chilled". Honestly, it's the reason why I prefer letting people read my poetry instead of performing it as spoken word. Spoken word is not necessarily in my wheelhouse. I feel like all my expressions bleed through the words on the page. It can be difficult to express those same emotions at times, in front of others.

Whatever it takes, make sure you celebrate yourself along the way of your author journey. Keep people around you who will support you and challenge you to celebrate yourself as well. An important aspect to keep in mind is that you have to remain your own competition. Watching the next person may discourage you at times.

There is a hidden aspect of any business and being an author is no different. If you compare yourself to other authors who may be winning awards or receiving accolades, it's easier to lose focus of your purpose. There are several awards out there that people pay to win. Also, for those that may not pay, they could be in categories where there is no competition. So, of course, that racks up another win.

Part of the downside of the wave of social media over the last

15 plus years is everyone shares highlight reels. Most people won't share their losses, disappoints or setbacks.

Who does that?

Almost no one.

People will share all the moments that make them look good and even envied by others. Don't believe the hype. Be your own encouragement and walk along your own path. The joy along the journey will be well worth it. Trust me.

Are you ready to execute that vision you've held on to for years?

Are you ready to make those financial sacrifices now to set yourself up for success later?

Are you ready to create and solidify plans to keep your goals on track?

I thought so. Let's go!

BRAIN PICKERS TO KEEP IN MIND:

- Make no comparisons to others.
- Surround yourself with people who will celebrate your milestones.
- Believe in your writing with conviction.
- No moment is too small to celebrate.
- Keep doing the right act to get the right attitude!

About the Author

CARLOS HARLEAUX is an author, poet, blogger/vlogger, publishing consultant and podcaster (tune into The Water Bearer Podcast on Thursdays on YouTube, Anchor, Spotify, Google Podcasts and Apple Podcasts). He resides in Dallas, Texas. He enjoys creative writing, live music, outdoor events, traveling and delicious food.

He is the author of several poetry books, including *Blurred Vision, Hindsight 20/20, Honesty Box, Commissioned to Love, Stingrays, Eleven: Things We Never Said, Cataracts* and the upcoming *Heads or Tails.*

Carlos's novels include *Fortune Cookie, No Cream in the Middle, When the Cookie Crumbles, A Swipe in the Wrong Direction, Only for One Night* and *Trigger Pointe.*

Visit peauxeticexpressions.com to learn more about Carlos, purchase his other books, read his blogs and get updates on upcoming projects.

Printed in the USA
CPSIA information can be obtained
at www.ICGtesting.com
JSHW060547230923
48797JS00012B/187

9 798218 084417